Electric Pressure Cooker Cookbook

Quick, Easy, and Healthy Electric Pressure Cooker Recipes for Your Family

Savannah Gibbs

Table of Contents

Chapter 1: Introducing the Electric Pressure Cooker

A new trend among people who eat healthy and enjoy cooking with minimal mess and time is the modern pressure cooker. This type of cooking instrument has been around for several decades, but the new models come to the market vastly improved and with health and convenience in mind. There's no need to spend hours in the kitchen, standing over multiple pots and pans.

How an Electric Pressure Cooker Works

If you're not familiar with the mechanics of an electric pressure cooker, they're pretty simple. The food is cooked inside a pot at high heat, and the steam that builds up inside that sealed environment conducts all the cooking. The heat and the pressure rise from the heating source throughout the pot. It's a clean, easy way to prepare food and eat well. Most cookers are sturdy and constructed of steel or aluminum. There are three parts to the cooker; the housing, the pot, and the lid that locks into place. You can most often find electric pressure cookers that are between three quarts and six quarts.

The Benefits of Using an Electric Pressure Cooker

The main benefit to cooking this way is that when you make your foods in a pressure cooker, they are retaining more of their nutrients than when you prepare them in other ways. Cooking times are shorter and there's less liquid involved. The longer you cook food, the more you're cooking off valuable ingredients such as vitamins, minerals, and proteins. Pressure cooking will not do that to your food. You'll reduce your cooking time by up to 70 percent, leaving all the flavor and the nutrients in what you eat. The temptation to simply order a pizza or throw something in the microwave instead of preparing a healthful meal will be eliminated. You always have time to throw something together in your cooker.

Another benefit is that the electric pressure cooker is environmentally sound. You're using less energy with this cooking tool than you would use with your oven or stovetop. The one-pot cooking technology will reduce your cleanup and your electric or gas bill. It also keeps your kitchen cooler.

How to Use an Electric Pressure Cooker

It's not difficult to use an electric pressure cooker. You'll simply load the food into the pot, add water, and lock the lid into place. Plug it in and set the timer and the heat regulator. The settings you choose will depend on what you're cooking, especially when you're preparing meat. When cooking is complete, you'll wait for the steam to cool down before you open the lid and remove your food.

You want to clean your pressure cooker every time you use it, and it's important not to put it in the dishwasher. Some pressure cookers have the pot piece that is dishwasher-safe, but consult your manual before you do that. Wipe out the pot with a wet sponge or rag, and use a mild soap if you need to scrape off or remove food bits. Never use anything abrasive that will scratch the cooker. Warm soapy water does the trick, and then you need to dry it completely.

Electric Pressure Cooking Safety

When you use a cooker like this, you're inviting extreme temperatures into your kitchen. That's going to help you achieve great tasting food, but it can be dangerous if you're not using the cooker correctly. Always follow the instructions in the manual of your specific pressure cooker. Never cook anything without the lid locked securely into place, and don't try to open it while it's cooking. Most cookers come with security features that won't allow you to open the lid when it's unsafe.

Check your equipment before and after you use it, to make sure everything is functional. Never overfill your pressure cooker. If you try to stuff too much food in there or you add too much liquid, you could be putting yourself at risk. Make sure you're releasing the stream and pressure in a safe way. The best way to do this is to simply wait for the lid to safely unlock. There may be a steam release valve to help you release the pressure faster, but watch your hands so you don't get burned.

Tips for Electric Pressure Cooking

To get the most effective use from your pressure cooker, make sure you use recipes that are specifically designed for this type of cooking tool. Make sure you use enough liquid when you're cooking, and don't try to fry anything in it because oil can damage the system. Use the best food ingredients you can find, and make sure you're willing to try new things.

This book presents you with 48 quick, easy, and healthy electric pressure cooker recipes for breakfast, chicken, turkey, beef, pork, seafood, soup, and desserts. All it requires you to do is to buy all ingredients, dump them in the pot, and allow it to work its magic.

Chapter 2: Electric Pressure Cooker Breakfast Recipes

When you're putting together electric pressure cooker breakfast recipes, you want to make sure you're preparing food that is healthy, easy to make, and fast. Whether you're someone who likes a big, hot breakfast or you prefer to grab and go, there are a number of recipes that will suit your needs and preferences.

Baked Egg Cups

Serves: 4

Ingredients:

4 ramekins

4 eggs

4 slices of ham

4 slices of cheese

4 sprigs of fresh rosemary

2 teaspoons olive oil

1 cup water

Directions:

1. Pour the water into the pressure cooker.

2. Lightly rub olive oil around the insides of each ramekin.

3. Break the eggs one at a time and add one egg to each of the ramekins, then the ham, and then the cheese.

4. Place the ramekins into a steamer basket and lower into the pressure cooker. Close and lock the lid and set the cooking pressure to low. Cook for four minutes.

5. Once the pressure has been released, remove the ramekins and sprinkle with fresh rosemary.

Almonds and Oats

Serves: 4

Ingredients:

1 cup steel cut oats

3½ cups coconut milk

1 tablespoon butter

¼ cup sliced almonds

¼ cup chocolate chips

¼ teaspoon salt

1 teaspoon cinnamon

1 teaspoon nutmeg

Directions:

1. Set your pressure cooker to a "sauté" setting and melt the butter in the pot.

2. Add the oats and toast for three minutes, stirring occasionally. You want them to smell toasty and begin to brown.

3. Add the milk, salt, cinnamon, and nutmeg.

4. Seal the lid, select a high pressure setting and set your timer for 10 minutes.

5. After the pressure has been released, carefully remove the lid and give everything a stir. Let it sit for five more minutes so the oats can thicken.

6. Add chocolate and almonds to the top and serve.

Rice Pudding Parfait

Serves: 6

Ingredients:

1 cup white rice

1½ cups water

2 cups milk, divided

½ cup sugar

2 eggs

½ teaspoon vanilla extract

1 cup raisins

¼ teaspoon salt

½ teaspoon cinnamon

½ cup blueberries

Directions:

1. Place the rice, water, and salt in the pressure cooker. Cook on high pressure for three minutes.

2. Let the natural pressure release, wait for 10 minutes, then open the pressure cooker.

3. Add one cup of the milk and the sugar and cinnamon. Stir everything together.

4. In a separate bowl, mix the eggs with the other cup of milk. Add the mixture to the pressure cooker.

5. Set the cooking function to "sauté" and stir while cooking for 3 minutes, until the mixture starts to boil.

6. Add the raisins and leave the mixture to cool and thicken for 5 minutes. Top with blueberries.

Gluten Free Buckwheat Porridge

Serves: 4

Ingredients:

1 cup buckwheat groats

3 cups coconut milk

1 large ripe banana, sliced

1 teaspoon cinnamon powder

1 teaspoon vanilla extract

¼ cup honey

¼ cup raisins

1 cup grated coconut

Some chopped walnuts

Directions:

1. Rinse the buckwheat with water and drain. Add to the pressure cooker. Pour in the coconut milk, sprinkle with the cinnamon powder, and add in the vanilla extract. Mix well.

2. Simmer this mixture for about 2-3 minutes.

3. Throw in the grated coconut, raisins, ripened banana, and honey, and cover the lid of the pressure cooker. Cook on high pressure for 10 minutes.

4. Release the pressure slowly and remove the porridge into a large bowl.

5. Garnish with some chopped walnuts and serve.

Home Fries with Cheese

Serves: 4

Ingredients:

1 pound small red potatoes, cut into cubes

1 cup low sodium chicken broth

1 tablespoon butter

¼ teaspoon salt

½ cup shredded parmesan cheese

1 teaspoon dried oregano

1 teaspoon dried rosemary

1 teaspoon dried parsley

Directions:

1. Melt the butter in the pressure cooker on "sauté." Add the potatoes and stir for about 5 minutes, until they are coated with butter.

2. Add the chicken broth and herbs. Close the lid and cook on high for 5 minutes.

3. Remove from heat and sprinkle the potatoes with salt and cheese.

Hard Boiled Eggs

Serves: 3

Ingredients:

6 eggs

1 cup ice

4 cups water

Directions:

1. Place a steamer basket in the pressure cooker pot. You can also use a rack if you don't have a basket.

2. Place the six fresh eggs in the basket and pour one cup of the water into the pressure cooker.

3. Close the lid and set the pressure cooker to high for 7 minutes. When cooking time is complete, carefully open the lid and remove the steamer basket.

4. Drop the eggs into a bowl that's filled with the remaining 3 cups of water and the ice. Allow them to cool for 5 minutes.

Breakfast Casserole

Serves: 4

Ingredients:

6 eggs

1 tablespoon butter

1 tablespoon milk

½ cup water

1 cup chopped ham

6 small red potatoes, chopped

Directions:

1. Melt the butter in the pressure cooker on "sauté."

2. In a bowl, beat the eggs with the milk. Add all the ingredients to the pressure cooker and seal the lid.

3. Cook on high pressure for 5 minutes.

Pumpkin Porridge

Serves: 4

Ingredients:

1 cup steel cut oats

½ cup pumpkin puree

3 cups water

1 tablespoon butter

¼ teaspoon salt

1 teaspoon brown sugar

Dash of cinnamon (or nutmeg)

Directions:

1. Melt butter in the pressure cooker pot on "sauté" for 2 minutes.

2. Add the oats, pumpkin, water, salt, and sugar.

3. Close the lid securely and cook on high pressure for 10 minutes.

4. Wait another 10 minutes for the natural pressure to release. Top the porridge with cinnamon or nutmeg and serve.

Chapter 3: Electric Pressure Cooker Chicken and Turkey Recipes

When you want to use your pressure cook to prepare high protein, low fat meals, consider building your plate around poultry. Chicken and turkey are tasty ways to eat healthy. These electric pressure cooker chicken and turkey recipes will give you the variety and the flavor you're looking for. Eating the same grilled piece of chicken meal after meal gets old fast. Liven things up a little with one of these choices.

Chicken Teriyaki

Serves: 4

Ingredients:

1½ pounds boneless chicken breast

1 can pineapple

1 cup chicken stock

¼ cup brown sugar

½ cup soy sauce

¼ cup apple cider vinegar

1 tablespoon ground ginger

1 tablespoon garlic powder

1 teaspoon black pepper

1 tablespoon cornstarch

1 tablespoon water

Directions:

1. In a bowl, combine the brown sugar, soy sauce, vinegar, ginger, garlic powder, and pepper until the sugar dissolves.

2. Place the chicken breasts in the pressure cooker and top with pineapple and chicken stock.

3. Pour the sugar mixture on top of that. Stir carefully to coat the chicken.

4. Set the pressure cooker to high pressure, and cook for 20 minutes.

5. Once the pressure is released, remove the chicken from the cooker but keep the liquid.

6. Add the cornstarch and water to the liquid and stir until it thickens. Use as a teriyaki sauce over the chicken.

Turkey Goulash

Serves: 4

Ingredients:

2 pounds ground turkey breast

1 15-ounce can of diced tomatoes

2 cloves garlic, chopped

1 red onion, sliced

1 red bell pepper, chopped

1 green bell pepper, chopped

1 cup chicken stock

1 tablespoon butter

Directions:

1. Heat the butter in the pressure cooker and add the ground turkey, cooking it on "sauté" for 5 minutes.

2. Add the tomatoes with their juices, the garlic, onion, peppers, and chicken stock.

3. Cover and set on high pressure. Cook for 15 minutes.

Whole Cooked Chicken

Serves: 6

Ingredients:

1 4-5 pound roaster chicken

1 cup of water

1 cup chicken stock

4 cloves garlic, whole

3 carrots, chopped

2 celery stalks, chopped

1 onion, quartered

Salt and pepper

Directions:

1. Rinse the chicken, pat dry with paper towels and season generously with salt and pepper. Place it in your pressure cooker on top of a cooking rack.

2. Add the vegetables and the water and chicken stock.

3. Cook for 25 minutes on high pressure.

Turkey Meatballs

Serves: 6

Ingredients:

1½ pounds ground turkey breast

1 cup breadcrumbs

1 onion, diced

2 cloves garlic, minced

¼ cup milk

1 teaspoon dried Italian seasoning

1 egg

2 tablespoons ketchup

1 can whole tomatoes

1 cup water

Directions:

1. Make the meatballs by combining the turkey breast, breadcrumbs, onion, garlic, milk, seasoning, egg, and ketchup. Use your hands to combine all those ingredients and form small balls.

2. Pour the whole tomatoes, with their juices, into the pressure cooker and add water. Mix the liquids together.

3. Add the meatballs. Cook on high pressure for 8 minutes.

4. Once the pressure is released, remove the meatballs and cover them with the sauce.

Pina Colada Chicken

Serves: 4

Ingredients:

2 pounds chicken thighs, cut into small pieces

1 cup diced pineapple

½ cup coconut cream

½ teaspoon salt

1 teaspoon ground cinnamon

¾ cup green onion, chopped

2 tablespoons desiccated coconut shavings

1 tablespoon arrowroot powder

1 tablespoon water

Directions:

1. Add all the above ingredients to your pressure cooker except for the green onions and mix well.

2. Cook for 15 minutes on high pressure.

3. Release the steam.

4. Add the arrowroot powder to a tablespoon of water, mix, and add it to the chicken. Let it simmer for a few minutes until it thickens.

5. Garnish with chopped green onions and serve.

Barbecue Chicken

Serves: 4

Ingredients:

2 chicken breasts, split in half

1 cup chicken stock

½ cup water

1 teaspoon nutmeg

1 teaspoon cinnamon

1 teaspoon ginger

1 teaspoon salt

1 teaspoon pepper

1 bottle barbecue sauce (use your favorite)

Directions:

1. Combine the salt, pepper, ginger, cinnamon and nutmeg in a small bowl and rub the mixture into the chicken breasts.

2. Place them in the pressure cooker and cover with the water and the chicken stock.

3. Set the cooker on high pressure and cook for 15 minutes.

4. When the pressure releases, remove the chicken and cover with barbecue sauce.

Simple Herb Turkey Breast

Serves: 6

Ingredients:

3 pounds turkey breast

1 can chicken broth (14 or 15 ounces)

1 red onion, quartered

3 stalks celery, roughly chopped

1 sprig fresh thyme

2 sprigs fresh rosemary

1 teaspoon dried basil

1 teaspoon dried oregano

Salt and pepper

Directions:

1. Season turkey breasts with salt, pepper, dried basil, and dried oregano.

2. Place a trivet at the bottom of the cooker and pour in the chicken broth. Add the rosemary and thyme.

3. Place the turkey on top, breast side up. Add the onion and celery.

4. Cook on high pressure for 20 minutes.

Sweet Garlic Chicken

Serves: 6

Ingredients:

3 pounds chicken drumsticks and thighs

2 cloves garlic, minced

2 teaspoons garlic Sriracha chili sauce

1 cup soy sauce

½ cup ketchup

1 cup honey

2 tablespoons brown sugar

2 tablespoons fresh basil, chopped

Salt and pepper

1 tablespoon cornstarch

1 tablespoon water

Directions:

1. In a bowl, whisk together the garlic, chili sauce, soy sauce, ketchup, honey, and brown sugar until the sugar dissolves. Pour the mixture into the pressure cooker.

2. Season the chicken pieces with salt and pepper, and place them into the cooker. Cook on high pressure for about 10 minutes.

3. Allow the pressure to release, and take the chicken out of the pot.

4. Stir in the cornstarch and the water, allowing the sauce to thicken. Pour it on top of the chicken before you serve.

Chapter 4: Electric Pressure Cooker Beef and Pork Recipes

A major part of any healthy and balanced eating program is protein. Beef and pork are packed with protein, and when you cook them in an electric pressure cooker, you get juicy, flavorful pieces of meat that taste delicious. These electric pressure cooker beef and pork recipes are sure to get your mouth watering. They are easy to prepare, mess-free and you'll be able to put them on the table in no time at all.

Best Barbeque Pork

Serves: 8

Ingredients:

4 pounds pork roast

2 cups water

1 bottle of your favorite bbq sauce

1 teaspoon garlic powder

1 teaspoon salt

1 teaspoon pepper

Directions:

1. Rub the roast with the garlic powder, salt, and pepper. Place it inside the pressure cooker and cover with the water.

2. Close the lid, cook on high pressure for 40 minutes.

3. Release the pressure and remove the pork roast from the cooker. Shred it and mix with the barbeque sauce.

4. Add a little of the liquid from the pressure cooker if you need to thin out the barbeque sauce at all.

Braised Beef Stew

Serves: 4

Ingredients:

1 pound beef, cut into chunks

2 cloves garlic

2 tablespoons olive oil

2 potatoes

1 Vidalia onion

2 carrots

1 14/15 ounce can of green beans

2 15-ounce cans diced tomatoes

2 tablespoons flour

½ cup water

1 teaspoon salt

1 teaspoon pepper

1 teaspoon dried oregano

Directions:

1. Toss the beef chunks in the olive oil until coated, then cover with the flour.

2. Place the beef in the pressure cooker and sauté the meat until it begins to brown.

3. Cut the potatoes, onion, and carrots into bit sized pieces and add to the pressure cooker.

4. Add the garlic and then the cans of green beans and tomatoes, with their liquid.

5. Season with salt, pepper, and oregano.

6. Pour the water into the cooker and then set the pressure on high. Lock the lid and cook for 15 minutes.

Super Sausage and Peppers

Serves: 4

Ingredients:

4 sweet Italian sausages

4 spicy Italian sausages

4 large bell peppers (any color)

1 15-ounce can diced tomatoes

1 15-ounce jar tomato sauce

1 cup water

1 red onion

4 cloves garlic, minced

2 tablespoons dried Italian seasoning

Directions:

1. Pour the tomatoes (with juices) and the tomato sauce into the pressure cooker.

2. Add the water, garlic, and Italian seasoning.

3. Chop the peppers and the onion into strips or chunks.

4. Add the sausages to the pressure cooker and top them with the peppers and onions.

5. Lock the lid into place and cook on high pressure for 20 minutes.

Maple Smoked Brisket

Serves: 4

Ingredients:

1½ pounds beef brisket

2 tablespoons brown sugar

2 teaspoons sea salt

1 teaspoon ground pepper

1 teaspoon mustard powder

1 tablespoon onion powder

½ teaspoon garlic powder

½ teaspoon paprika powder

1 tablespoon olive oil

2 cups of chicken broth

1 tablespoon liquid smoke

Some fresh thyme leaves

Directions:

1. If the brisket is refrigerated, ensure you take it out and let it sit at room temperature for about 30 minutes.

2. In a bowl, combine brown sugar, sea salt, ground pepper, mustard powder, onion powder, garlic powder, and paprika powder.

3. Lay the brisket on a tray. Generously coat the meat with the above mixture.

4. Grease the bottom of the pressure cooker with olive oil. Heat for about 3 minutes on "sauté" setting.

5. Transfer the brisket to the pressure cooker and cook on both sides until golden brown. Make sure you don't burn the brisket while doing this.

6. Next, pour the chicken broth on top of the brisket, followed by liquid smoke. Close the lid, and cook for 50 minutes on high pressure.

7. Serve with some thyme leaves on top.

Corned Beef and Cabbage

Serves: 4

Ingredients:

3 pounds corned beef

4 cups beef broth

3 cups water

2 cloves garlic, minced

3 tablespoons spicy mustard

1 teaspoon whole peppercorns

1 head of cabbage, shredded

4 carrots, chopped

2 potatoes, cut into chunks

Directions:

1. Rinse the corned beef and place it in the pressure cooker on a rack, with the fat part of the meat facing up. Cover with broth and water.

2. Add the garlic, mustard, and peppercorns.

3. Cover the pressure cooker and set the pressure to high. Cook for 45 minutes.

4. While it's cooking, place the cabbage, carrots, and potatoes into a basket.

5. When the corned beef is done, remove it carefully and place the basket of veggies into the same cooking liquid. Cook on high pressure for three minutes.

Pork Chops with Mushrooms

Serves: 4

Ingredients:

4 thick pork chops

2 tablespoons olive oil

1 15-ounce can of tomato soup

1 bell pepper, chopped

1 red onion, chopped

6 carrots, chopped

6 small red potatoes

2 cups button mushrooms, chopped

Directions:

1. Rub the pork chops with olive oil and sauté in the pressure cooker until they begin to brown.

2. Add peppers, onions, carrots, potatoes, and mushrooms.

3. Add the tomato soup. Secure the lid and cook on high pressure for about 15 minutes.

Sesame Beef & Broccoli

Serves: 4

Ingredients:

1 pound beef roast

2 tablespoons sesame oil

1 onion, chopped

3 cloves garlic, minced

1 cup beef broth

½ cup soy sauce

1/3 cup brown sugar

½ teaspoon red pepper flakes

1 pound broccoli

¼ cup peanuts

2 tablespoons sesame seeds

Salt and pepper

Directions:

1. Coat the beef with sesame oil and season with salt and pepper, then place in the pressure cooker to brown.

2. Add onion and garlic and sauté for 2 minutes.

3. Add broth, brown sugar, soy sauce, and red pepper flakes. Cook another two minutes.

4. Cover the pressure cook and set to high. Cook for 10 minutes.

5. Steam the broccoli while the beef cooks, in the microwave or stovetop.

6. After the pressure has been released, toss it all together.

Pork Ribs

Serves: 4

Ingredients:

2 pounds boneless pork ribs

1 tablespoon olive oil

3 tablespoons ketchup

1 teaspoon dried onion powder

1 teaspoon garlic salt

1 teaspoon pepper

1 teaspoon paprika

1 cup water

4 teaspoons white vinegar

1 tablespoon Worcestershire sauce

1 tablespoon Dijon mustard

Directions:

1. Coat the ribs in the oil and brown in the pressure cooker for about 5 minutes.

2. Sprinkle with onion powder, garlic salt, pepper, and paprika.

3. Add water, ketchup, vinegar, Worcestershire sauce, and mustard.

4. Cover and cook on high pressure for 15 minutes.

Chapter 5: Electric Pressure Cooker Seafood Recipes

Many people love seafood, and incorporating more fish into your diet is a great way to get protein and healthy fats without adding a lot of calories and saturated fats. Sometimes, cooking fish can seem boring; either you grill it, pan fry it or bake it with the requisite lemon and seasonings. The electric pressure cooker offers a new option. These electric pressure cooker seafood recipes will have you enjoying fish in a whole new way. Cooking it will be almost as enjoyable as eating it.

Steamed Salmon

Serves: 4

Ingredients:

4 salmon filets

2 cups water

4 Roma tomatoes

2 lemons

½ cup chopped shallots

4 sprigs fresh rosemary

Salt and pepper

Directions:

1. Slice the tomatoes and the lemons.

2. Make two foil pouches with two pieces of salmon each.

3. Lay the salmon down on the foil and cover with salt and pepper, olive oil, a layer of tomatoes, a layer of lemons, a sprinkle of shallots and a sprig of rosemary. Fold up the foil so it creates a secure little package.

4. Pour the water into the pressure cooker and place the salmon into the steamer basket.

5. Cook on low pressure for 15 minutes.

6. When the pressure has released, carefully unfold the packets.

Coconut Fish Curry

Serves: 5

Ingredients:

1½ pounds fish steak (cut into small pieces)
1 tablespoon coconut oil
1 cup cherry tomatoes
2 small green chilies, slit open
2 medium onions, sliced
2 garlic cloves, minced
1 teaspoon coriander powder
2 teaspoons ground cumin
¼ teaspoon turmeric
Some curry leaves
1 teaspoon chili powder
3 tablespoons curry powder
2 cups coconut milk
¾ teaspoon salt
1 tablespoon lemon juice
1 teaspoon minced ginger

Directions:

1. Set the pressure cooker to "sauté" and heat the coconut oil.

2. Add curry leaves, minced ginger, garlic, and sliced onion and fry for 2-3 minutes.

3. Add the turmeric powder, ground cumin, and coriander powder and mix well.

4. Slide in the chilies and cherry tomatoes and sauté for another 2 minutes.

5. Pour in the coconut milk, add the salt and lemon juice, and bring to a boil.

6. Transfer the fish steaks and give the mixture a stir.

7. Close the lid and cook for 5-7 minutes on high pressure.

8. Serve hot.

Ginger-Lemon Haddock

Serves: 4

Ingredients:

4 filets of haddock

2 lemons

1-inch piece of fresh ginger, chopped

4 green onions

1 cup white wine

Salt and pepper to taste

2 tablespoons olive oil

Directions:

1. Massage the olive oil into the fish filets and sprinkle them with salt and pepper.

2. Juice your lemons and zest one of them. Add that to the pressure cooker with the wine, onions, and ginger.

3. Place the fish in the steamer basket and lower it to the liquid.

4. Close the lid and cook on high pressure for 8 minutes.

5. When the pressure is released, remove the fish and serve on rice or with a big salad.

Cod with Parsley and Piselli

Serves: 4

Ingredients:

1 pound cod, cut into 4 filets

1 bag (10 ounces) frozen peas

1 cup fresh parsley

1 cup white wine

2 garlic cloves, smashed

1 teaspoon paprika

1 teaspoon oregano

1 sprig fresh rosemary

Directions:

1. In a small bowl, stir the wine and the herbs and spices together until blended. Pour the liquid into the pressure cooker and add the frozen peas.

2. Place the fish into the steamer basket and close the lid.

3. Cook on high pressure for 5 minutes.

4. The peas will be mushy and soft, so plate those first and serve the fish on top.

Spicy Shrimp

Serves: 4

Ingredients:

1 pound frozen shrimp, peeled and deveined

1 lemon, juiced

1 teaspoon black pepper

1 teaspoon white pepper

1 teaspoon cayenne pepper

1 can diced tomatoes (14-15 ounces)

1 jalapeno pepper, minced

2 cloves garlic, minced

1 sweet onion, minced

Directions:

1. Pour the tomatoes and juices into the pressure cooker.

2. Add the lemon juice, garlic, and onion and stir.

3. Allow the frozen shrimp to rest at room temperature for 15 minutes. Then, add them to the pressure cooker.

4. Add the jalapeno and the black, white, and cayenne peppers.

5. Mix everything. Cook on high pressure for 5 minutes.

Mediterranean Calamari

Serves: 6

Ingredients:

2 pounds calamari or squid, chopped

2 tablespoons olive oil

1 red onion, sliced

3 cloves of garlic, chopped

1 cup red wine

3 stalks of celery, chopped

1 can (28 ounces) crushed tomatoes

3 sprigs fresh rosemary

½ cup Italian parsley, chopped

Salt and pepper

Directions:

1. Toss the calamari pieces in olive oil and salt and pepper.

2. To the pressure cooker, add the wine, tomatoes with their juices, celery, rosemary, garlic, and red onion.

3. Place the calamari in the steamer basket and lower it to the liquid. Cook on high pressure for 4 minutes.

4. Remove the fish once the pressure has eased and sprinkle with fresh parsley.

Fish Chowder

Serves: 6

Ingredients:

1 pound frozen tilapia filets

1 cup chicken broth

1 cup water

1 cup milk

1 cup heavy cream

6 red potatoes, chopped

1 cup frozen salad shrimp, peeled and deveined

3 stalks of celery, chopped

4 carrots, chopped

1 tablespoon dried thyme

1 tablespoon dried parsley

Directions:

1. Chop up the tilapia into small, bite-size pieces. Add it to the pressure cooker with the salad shrimp, chicken broth, milk, water, potatoes, celery, and carrots.

2. Add the thyme and parsley and stir, until combined.

3. Cook in the pressure cooker on high pressure for 10 minutes.

4. Let the pressure release and lift the lid. Stir in the heavy cream until everything in the pot thickens.

Steamed Mussels

Serves: 3

Ingredients:

3 pounds fresh mussels, cleaned and rinsed

1 can diced tomatoes (14 ounces)

1 cup white wine

1 tablespoon pepper

1 tablespoon dried parsley

Directions:

1. Pour the tomatoes into the pressure cooker with the juices and add the wine. Stir together and add the pepper and parsley.

2. Place the mussels in the steamer basket and cook on high pressure for 3 minutes.

3. Remove the lid when the pressure is released and cover the mussels with the tomato and wine sauce.

4. Serve with garlic bread.

Chapter 6: Electric Pressure Cooker Soup Recipes

With these electric pressure cooker soup recipes, you'll never have to open a can of soup again. You'll be able to make fresh, delicious soups and stews within minutes. Whether you want a light lunch or a hearty meal served with crusty bread alongside a sandwich or a salad, these soups are bound to leave you feeling well-fed. They are easy and they're fun to try.

Smoky Chicken Soup

Serves: 4

Ingredients:

2 tablespoons olive oil, divided

1 medium onion, diced

2 garlic cloves, minced

4 cups chicken broth

3 chicken breasts

4 large tomatoes, diced

2 tablespoons thick tomato paste

¾ tablespoon chili powder

½ teaspoon smoked paprika powder

1 teaspoon sea salt

Ground pepper to taste

1 tablespoon lime juice

Some freshly chopped cilantro and sour cream for topping

Directions:

1. Set the pressure cooker to "sauté" and heat 1 tablespoon olive oil.

2. Add minced garlic and onion and sauté until the onion turns slightly golden brown.

3. Toss in the diced tomatoes and tomato paste and cook for about 3 minutes.

4. Add the chili powder, smoked paprika powder, sea salt, and ground pepper, and give it a mix.

5. Heat 1 tablespoon olive oil in another pan over medium heat. Place the chicken breasts in it and cook until slightly brown on both sides.

6. Transfer the chicken breasts to the pressure cooker, followed by 4 cups of chicken broth.

8. Add the lime juice and close the lid. Cook for 10 minutes on high pressure.

9. Serve with some cilantro and sour cream on top.

Baked Potato Soup

Serves: 6

Ingredients:

6 cups of potatoes, peeled and cubed

2 tablespoons butter

½ cup chopped shallots

4 cups of chicken broth

6 slices bacon, cooked and cooled

1 cup shredded cheddar cheese

1 cup shredded mozzarella cheese

2 tablespoons dried parsley

1 teaspoon cayenne pepper

2 tablespoons cornstarch

2 tablespoons water

2 cups heavy cream

Salt and pepper

Directions:

1. Melt the butter in the pressure cooker and add the shallots, stirring until coated.

2. Add 2 cups of the chicken broth, the parsley, cayenne pepper, and salt and pepper. Stir.

3. Put the potatoes in a steamer basket and attach the lid. Cook on high pressure for 5 minutes.

4. Release the pressure, and remove the potatoes.

5. Add the cheese to the mixture in the pressure cooker and stir until melted.

6. Add the remaining chicken broth and the heavy cream.

7. In a small bowl, mix the cornstarch and water together and add it to the pot.

8. Toss in the bacon and the cooked potatoes.

Creamy Tomato Soup

Serves: 4

Ingredients:

6 large tomatoes

1 cup water

1 cup heavy cream

½ cup fresh basil leaves, chopped

1 tablespoon dried oregano

1 teaspoon salt

1 teaspoon white pepper

Directions:

1. Cut the tomatoes into halves and place them in the pressure cooker. Add one cup of water.

2. Cook on high pressure for 5 minutes and allow pot to return to normal pressure.

3. Lift the lid and use an immersion blender to achieve a smooth consistency.

4. Add the cream, herbs, and salt and pepper to taste.

Ham and Bean Soup

Serves: 4

Ingredients:

1 pound dried black beans (or any favorite bean)

1 cup water

1 can (14/15 ounces) diced tomatoes

1 small onion, chopped

1 cup frozen peas

1 clove garlic

2 cups cubed cooked ham

Directions:

1. Put the dried beans in the pressure cooker and cover with water and tomatoes, in their juices. Add the onion, peas, and garlic.

2. Cook on high pressure for 25 minutes and allow the pressure to ease.

3. Open the pot and stir in the cubed ham.

Beef and Veggie Stew

Serves: 4

Ingredients:

½ pound beef cut into small pieces

1 large potato, peeled and diced

2 tablespoons olive oil

1 cup water

½ red onion, diced

2 stalks celery, chopped

2 carrots, chopped

2 cups kale

1 can (14/15 ounces) diced tomatoes

4 cups beef broth

1 cup frozen green beans

1 cup frozen corn

1 teaspoon cumin

1 teaspoon paprika

Salt and pepper

Directions:

1. Toss the beef chunks in the olive oil and heat in the pressure cooker until they begin to brown.

2. Add the potato, onion, celery, carrots, kale, green beans, and corn.

3. Add the water, broth, and the tomatoes with their juices.

4. Stir in the cumin and paprika.

5. Cook on high pressure for 30 minutes and sprinkle with salt and pepper to taste.

Chicken Noodle Soup

Serves: 6

Ingredients:

2 chicken breasts

6 cups chicken stock

2 tablespoons olive oil

3 carrots, chopped

3 celery stalks, chopped

1 cup frozen peas

1 cup frozen corn

2 cups egg noodles

¼ cup fresh parsley

Salt and pepper

Directions:

1. Chop the chicken breast into small, bite sized pieces and toss with olive oil. Put it in the pressure cooker to brown for about 5 minutes.

2. Add the carrots and celery as well as the salt and pepper. Let everything cook for 2 more minutes.

3. Then, add the chicken stock, the frozen peas, and corn and the egg noodles. Stir everything together.

4. Seal the pressure cooker lid and cook on high pressure for 8 minutes.

5. When the pressure reduces, sprinkle with parsley and serve.

Split Pea Soup

Serves: 4

Ingredients:

1 cup dried split peas

2 cups chicken stock

4 slices Canadian bacon, chopped

1 onion, sliced

2 small red potatoes, chopped

2 cloves garlic, minced

½ cup cream

2 tablespoons fresh parsley

Salt and pepper

Directions:

1. Heat the bacon in the pressure cooker and as fat comes off the bacon, stir in the onion and garlic.

2. Add the chicken stock and the potatoes. Stir in the cream and the peas until everything is combined.

3. Cook for 15 minutes on high pressure.

4. Season with salt and pepper and parsley.

Hot and Sour Soup

Serves: 4

Ingredients:

½ pound chicken breast, cut into cubes

1 tablespoon sesame oil

3 cups chicken stock

2 tablespoons fresh ginger, grated

1 tablespoon freshly squeezed lime juice

1 whole chili pepper, sliced and seeded

1 tomato, chopped

½ cup fresh mushrooms, sliced

2 tablespoons fish sauce

2 tablespoons fresh cilantro

Directions:

1. Toss the chicken pieces in the sesame oil and heat in the pressure cooker for 5 minutes.

2. Add the chicken stock, ginger, lime juice, chili pepper, tomato, and mushrooms. Stir together.

3. Cook on high pressure for 10 minutes.

4. Once pressure is released, stir in the fish sauce and the cilantro.

Chapter 7: Electric Pressure Cooker Dessert Recipes

Every good meal ends with a dessert, and whether you like yours simple or decadent, it's possible to create an impressive final course with your electric pressure cooker. Your mouth will water when you start gathering the ingredients for these electric pressure cooker dessert recipes. With everything from chocolate to wine to cream - you're bound to find a favorite and make it a weekly treat.

Green Tea Coconut Crème Brûlée

Serves: 4

Ingredients:

1 tablespoon green tea powder

1½ cups whole cream

1 cup coconut milk (whole fat)

1½ teaspoons vanilla extract

¼ teaspoon salt

6 large egg yolks

8 tablespoons brown sugar, divided

Boiling water

Directions:

1. In a large bowl, combine coconut milk, cream, vanilla extract, salt, and mix well.

2. Heat this mixture in a small saucepan while continuously stirring.

3. In another bowl, whisk the egg yolks along with the brown sugar until all ingredients are blended.

4. Pour the cream mixture into the bowl and stir well.

5. Transfer the mixture to small ramekins or heatproof bowls. Be sure to fill only ¾ of the bowl with the mixture, so it leaves room for rising.

6. Add some boiling water to the pressure cooker and set on a trivet. Place the ramekins on it and close the lid.

7. Cook for 5 minutes on high pressure and wait for the pressure to release on its own.

8. Refrigerate the ramekins for at least 4 hours.

9. Remove the ramekins and sprinkle some sugar on top. With the help of a blowtorch, melt the sugar until it turns brown, and serve.

Wine-Soaked Pears

Serves: 6

Ingredients:

1 cup red wine

6 Anjou pears

1 vanilla bean

1 teaspoon cinnamon

2 whole cloves

¼ cup brown sugar

Directions:

1. Place the wine, vanilla, cinnamon, cloves, and sugar in the pressure cooker. Stir to combine everything.

2. Peel the skin off the pears, but leave the stems on. Place them in the wine mixture, so that they are standing.

3. Cook on low pressure for 7 minutes.

Chocolate Cake with Jam

Serves: 8

Ingredients:

1½ cups flour

4 tablespoons cocoa powder

¼ cup blackberry jam

1 cup milk

1 tablespoon salted butter, melted

¾ cup sugar

2 eggs

1 teaspoon baking powder

2 tablespoons confectioner's sugar

Directions:

1. In a bowl, sift together flour, cocoa powder, and baking powder.

2. In a separate bowl, whisk the eggs with the sugar and the melted butter. Stir in the jam until the ingredients are combined.

3. Slowly combine the flour mixture with the wet mixture.

4. Add milk. Pour into a greased pan and place it into the pressure cooker on a trivet.

5. Cook on low pressure for 30 minutes.

6. Sprinkle with confectioner's sugar once the cake has cooled.

Nutty Fudge Pieces

Serves: 2 dozen fudge pieces

Ingredients:

1 12-ounce package of semi sweet chocolate chips

1 14-ounce can of condensed milk

½ cup walnuts

½ cup almonds

1 teaspoon vanilla

2 cups water

Directions:

1. Combine the milk and chocolate chips in a small or medium bowl (make sure it will fit in your pressure cooker). Cover the bowl with aluminum foil.

2. Pour the water into the pressure cooker and set the rack so you can place the bowl on top of it in the cooker. Cook on high pressure for 5 minutes.

3. Remove the bowl once the pressure has abated and take the foil off the bowl. Stir in the nuts and vanilla until everything is combined.

4. Drop in unformed balls onto wax paper and allow to cool.

Sweet Rice Pudding

Serves: 6

Ingredients:

1 cup uncooked long grain rice

¼ cup heavy cream

¼ cup sugar

1 cup water

2 cups milk

1 teaspoon vanilla

1 teaspoon cinnamon

1 teaspoon nutmeg

1 egg

½ teaspoon salt

1 tablespoon butter

Directions:

1. Melt the butter in the pressure cooker and add the rice, stirring to coat.

2. Add water, salt, milk, and sugar. Press the lid into place and cook on high pressure for 7 minutes.

3. While it's cooking, mix the egg, cream, and vanilla in a separate bowl. Add a little bit of the hot cooking liquid from the pressure cooker to the egg mixture to temper it.

4. After you do this successfully, add the egg mixture to the pressure cooker.

5. Cook uncovered for about 5 minutes, until it begins to bubble.

6. Stir while it cools and sprinkle cinnamon and nutmeg on top.

Chocolate Mousse with Raspberries

Serves: 8

Ingredients:

1 cup heavy cream

1 cup whole milk

¼ cup super-fine sugar

12 ounces dark cooking chocolate

6 egg yolks

1 teaspoon vanilla extract

1 tablespoon cocoa powder

6 fresh raspberries

2 cups water

Directions:

1. Stir the cream, milk, and sugar in a saucepan on low heat until sugar dissolves. Add the chocolate pieces.

2. Whisk the egg yolks until they become thick and slowly add to the chocolate. Add the vanilla.

3. Pour the chocolate mixture into a greased ovenproof dish. Cover with foil.

4. Add the water to the pressure cooker and place the dish on a trivet. Close the lid and cook on low pressure for 20 minutes.

5. Once it has cooled, remove the dish. Dust with cocoa powder and place the raspberries in the mousse.

Apples A La Mode

Serves: 4

Ingredients:

4 red delicious apples

1 lemon

2 cups grape juice

¼ cup strawberry jelly

1 teaspoon pepper

½ vanilla bean

¼ cup crushed walnuts

4 cups ice cream

Directions:

1. Pour the juice and jelly into the pressure cooker. Heat over sauté, while stirring until the jelly breaks down.

2. Grate the rind off the lemon and then cut the lemon in half and squeeze the juice into the pressure cooker. Add the rind.

3. Core the apples from the bottom, so the form stays intact. Coat the apples in the jelly mixture and then wrap them in aluminum foil.

4. Place the apples in a steamer basket. Add the pepper and vanilla to the cooker and lower the apples.

5. Cook on high pressure for 10 minutes.

6. Once cool and pressure is released, unwrap the apples and cover them with ice cream and walnuts.

Chunky Applesauce

Serves: 4

Ingredients:

10 apples, cored, peeled and cut into chunks

¼ cup apple juice

¼ cup water

¼ cup sugar

2 teaspoons ground cinnamon

Directions:

1. Place the apples, liquid, sugar, and cinnamon in your pressure cooker. Close the lid and cook for 5 minutes on high pressure.

2. When pressure releases, stir until apples break down to the level of consistency you prefer.

Conclusion

Cooking with an electric pressure cooker is a great way to prepare hot foods, even when you're in a hurry. There's no longer any need to rely on fast but unhealthy foods. Enjoy incorporating these easy, delicious, and healthy recipes into your everyday eating.

Finally, I want to thank you for reading my book. If you enjoyed the book, please take the time to share your thoughts and post a review on the Electric Pressure Cooker Cookbook: Quick, Easy, and Healthy Electric Pressure Cooker Recipes for Your Family Amazon book page. It would be greatly appreciated!

Best wishes,

Savannah Gibbs

Check Out My Other Books

Slow Cooker Cookbook: Easy, Delicious, and Healthy Slow Cooker Recipes for Your Family
https://www.amazon.com/dp/B06XCGQFP3/

Essential Oils for Beginners: 56 Best Essential Oil Recipes for Your Health and Beauty
https://www.amazon.com/dp/B01MXYTEW7/

Made in the USA
Lexington, KY
30 September 2018